Meditations and Rituals for Conscious Living:

A REFLECTIVE MEDITATION PROCESS

D1431282

NANCY J. NAPIER   CAROLYN M. TRICOMI

Cover & Book Design by:
Rebecca L. Spath, Pathwork Publications, New York, N.Y.

For ordering information please contact:
Lotus Blossom Press
P.O. Box 153
New York, New York 10024

ISBN# -0-9658191-3-2

MONTHLY THEMES

January
STILLNESS

February
WHOLENESS

March
COMPASSION & LOVINGKINDNESS

April
GETTING GROUNDED

May
MINDFULNESS

June
GRATITUDE & GENEROSITY

July
ONENESS

August
INTENTION

September
CREATING POSSIBILITY & SYNCHRONICITY

October
PARADOX

November
ACTIVE SURRENDER

December
LIVING CONSCIOUSLY

*This book is dedicated to
our beloveds here and our Beloveds there.*

FROM THE AUTHORS

Two heads really are better than one, and this book reflects, on every page, a synthesis of the contributions of both Carolyn and Nancy. It's a Napier-Tricomi/Tricomi-Napier collaboration and something more -- a reflection of the inspiration we received from the invisible realms, resulting in a whole that is definitely greater than the sum of its parts.

The pleasure of creating the meditations and rituals came from the process of combining our ideas and inspirations to arrive at a book neither of us would have written on our own. We think the outcome is part of, and reflects, the larger, collective shift that is characteristic of the movement from an emphasis on individual expression to an emphasis on group cooperation.

PREFACE TO THE 2004 EDITION

Much has happened in our global community since we first published this book in 2000. We offer this new edition as a way for people to actively and consciously connect with their spiritual lives. More than ever, we hope it contributes to expanding the capacity to maintain equanimity in the presence of uncertainty. As the world moves through dramatic events, there is a moment-to-moment opportunity for each of us to find an internal stance of peace and still ness in the present moment. Achieving ever-increasing levels of equanimity and peace in ourselves transcends our individual field of being and touches those in our personal lives, our communities, and the collective that is our human family.

BEGINNING THE JOURNEY:
An Invitation into the Experience of Reflective Meditation

This book offers a meditation process for conscious living. It invites you to reflect on weekly meditations that allow you to deepen your understanding of themes and practices that bring spiritual experience to life.

Each month presents a meditation theme that develops week by week. Early reflections become the foundation for expanding your experience of the monthly theme. Each week deepens your understanding of the theme and the month ends with a ritual that allows you to bring your meditation to life in practical and grounded ways.

Whereas in mindfulness meditation the goal is to observe what is moving through awareness without attachment, reflective meditation is a process of deep exploration without attachment, a process of deep exploration of ideas and concepts. In this way your ever-deepening contemplation of a particular theme allows it to enter your experience and understanding through images, related concepts, and intuitive insight.

The combination of reflective meditation and ritual provides a foundation for living each day consciously and with an open heart, creating a more alive and vital connection to the world, and to the sacred.

Setting the Space
To begin your practice of reflective meditation, find a place

where you have the least amount of distraction, where you can return preferably at the same time of the day each time you meditate. Sit on the floor with your legs crossed or in a chair with your feet on the floor, or in any other position that allows your back to be straight and your body relaxed with your mind alert. You might have paper and pen nearby, in case you want to take notes on the subject of your meditation. If you are an experienced meditator, meditate for 20 minutes once a day. If you are just beginning, you may find that 20 minutes is too long a time to concentrate on a chosen subject. Begin with whatever period of time feels comfortable to you -- starting with five minutes or more -- until you work up to a 20 minute meditation. It's fine to give more time to the process if you want to do so.

The Importance of Ritual and Ceremony

While we use the term *ritual* to describe the activities associated with each month's meditative theme, we could as easily use the word *ceremony.* For some people, rituals are those activities handed down through a particular tradition which, in themselves, are imbued with power. Ceremonies, then, are those spontaneous creations that celebrate or express some moment, idea, person, or event. For us, the word ritual conveys the conscious, empowered quality that we experience when we participate in symbolic activities. We chose this word because of the power it implies. . . that something real is happening when you participate in this kind of activity. Whichever word most closely matches your experience is fine. The goal is to create and participate in activities that translate spiritual ideas into actual behavior.

Whether called ritual or ceremony, these mindfully chosen activities offer you a means by which you can consciously:

- *bring attention and focus to your experience;*
- *move ideas from abstract into concrete reality;*

- *acknowledge internal experiences as external expression;*
- *mark that something - a person, place, belief - is significant to you, is worth honoring in a sacred, mindful way;*
- *slow down and become conscious of how you interact with your world and your day-to-day life;*
- *experience real acts that affect you and your world, that emerge from and invoke, in themselves, an open heart and an enhanced connection to the world of meaning, to the sacred.*

Rituals may be as simple as mindfully lighting a candle that is safely contained in an appropriate holder, or as complex as a tea ceremony. The depth and complexity of the ritual is determined by what it serves and what you seek to express and translate through participating in it.

For many people, daily rituals of meditation take place in front of an altar. An altar is a focal point, a place to focus your attention to engage in worship, ritual, or meditation. It may be on a tabletop, on the floor, on the ground outdoors. An altar generally contains objects that are sacred to you, that represent spiritually meaningful teachers and qualities. Objects on an altar may include photographs, incense, candles, feathers, crystals, or *any* object that has spiritual significance. Many of the rituals we will share with you suggest you bring sacred objects to your altar. Remove or replace these objects as you feel called to do so.

Each month's ritual may be used at the end of the month, after you've spent time with the theme. If it feels more powerful to you, though, allow yourself to experience the ritual at any time during the month when you are called to do so. Also, these are *suggestions* of what a ritual might be. Feel free to change them or create your own. Most important is to engage in experiences that speak to you -- to your intention, personal style, and unique relationship to the sacred.

To spend a week contemplating one idea, and then to deepen that idea over a period of three more weeks, gives you an opportunity to go beyond your initial understanding. It allows enough time for you to discover meanings that you may not have anticipated would emerge from your exploration. It is our expectation that by meditating on the concepts encompassed in each month's meditation theme, by the end of the year you will discover that your spiritual experience and understanding have deepened and expanded in ways that you may not have expected when you initially began the process.

January

STILLNESS

STILLNESS

January 1- 8

Stillness is the ground of being from which all else emerges. It is within and behind every breath, every thought, every action. It is my starting point, my resting place, the home base to which I can return again and again.

January 9-16

In stillness I notice how time and space disappear. All there is is the present moment and my willingness to listen. . . to allow the stillness to speak.

January 17 – 23

The stillness takes me into a realm of conscious awareness that transcends my identity as body or mind. Stillness offers an experience of *being* and a recognition that *my* being . . . *my* essence. . . is part of *all Being, all Essence.*

STILLNESS

January 24-31

The more I get to know stillness, I recognize
it as the cornerstone of my spiritual practice,
the ever-present pathway home.

ಇಂಜ

Ritual: Stillness

Find an object that represents the stillpoint, the "held moment" in which you experience stillness. It may be a photograph, a rock, a leaf, or any object that conveys the experience of the quiet focus that emerges spontaneously when you become aware of the space between the inbreath and the outbreath.

Next, light a candle in preparation for putting your object on the altar. Carefully place the object on the altar and attune yourself to it for a few moments. Through this attunement, enter the stillness even more fully for whatever period of time you wish.

When you are finished, complete the ritual by blowing out the candle and thanking the object for its presence and contribution to your experience of stillness.

February

WHOLENESS

WHOLENESS

February 1-7

From stillness I move into the recognition that
everything that is, anywhere and everywhere,
is a part of me, that separation is an illusion –
and that *wholeness* is the ever-present reality.

WHOLENESS

February 8 – 14

In a world of wholeness, light reveals shadow as shadow gives shape to light. Shadows offer definition, distinction, form and depth. In the wholeness of light and dark, love and fear, grief and joy, life is enriched by the contribution that each experience brings.

೪ು೦೪

WHOLENESS

February 15 – 21

In my personal life, I recognize that I, too, am shaped and deepened by the interplay of light and shadow. Recognizing my capacity to engage and move through difficult emotions and experiences, I embrace my whole self.

WHOLENESS

February 22 – 28

Wholeness invites me to integrate all of life's experiences, and to embrace them as a teaching and an opportunity for growth. No experience can be left outside the whole, for all that is expressed in human form also lives in me.

ଧଓ୪

Ritual: Wholeness

Choose a bowl that fits on your altar. Place within it objects that, at this moment in time, represent for you the wholeness of life -- the light and the dark, life and death, joy and sadness, love and hate. As you look at the bowl filled with these objects, say aloud: *"In a world of wholeness, my life is enriched by the contribution that each experience brings."*

End the ritual by honoring and thanking each object for its participation in your exploration and experience of wholeness.

March

COMPASSION
AND
LOVINGKINDNESS

March 1 - 8

From wholeness I recognize myself in all people. This recognition awakens compassion within me, and I remember that all beings seek to be free from suffering. With lovingkindness, I explore my experience of wishing that freedom for myself and others.

୫୦୪ଓ

March 9 – 16

To live with compassion challenges me to recognize and release judging myself and others. As I drop my judgments, I notice how I soften into the opening of my heart.

૭૦૦૪

COMPASSION & LOVINGKINDNESS

March 17 - 23

An open heart naturally extends itself to touch all beings with compassion. As my heart opens, I remember that: judgement separates . . . compassion embraces. . . lovingkindness blesses.

∞೦೮౩

COMPASSION & LOVINGKINDNESS

March 24 - 31

Compassion calls me forth into acts of lovingkindness.

ೞಞ

Ritual: Compassion & Lovingkindness

Begin your day with an intention to do random acts of lovingkindness. Light a candle and imagine that the flame of the candle represents the flame of love that lives in your heart. As you look at the flame, invite your heart to open. Then, affirm out loud your intention and willingness to bring your open heart into the world each day in acts of generosity, compassion, and lovingkindness.

As you complete the ritual, blow out the candle and convey gratitude to yourself for whatever degree of willingness you experience to live with an open heart.

April

GETTING GROUNDED

GETTING GROUNDED

April 1 – 7

My body is the vehicle by which I am grounded in my everyday experience. When I bring compassion and lovingkindness to my body, I honor the irreplaceable gifts it brings me.

80 03

GETTING GROUNDED

April 8 – 15

My breath brings awareness into my body. Being in my body connects me to the present moment. Being grounded in the present moment allows me to be conscious of my choices and the actions I take.

୫୦୧୪

GETTING GROUNDED

April 16 – 22

When I am anchored securely in my body, my consciousness is free to explore expanded states and spiritual realms. No matter where my awareness goes, I return to the grounding presence of my physical self.

৪০০৪

GETTING GROUNDED

April 23 – 30

When I experience myself as spirit in form, I recognize all forms as sacred expressions of spirit. When I am grounded in this understanding, I realize that all aspects of everyday life are spirit in action.

൫൰

Ritual: Getting Grounded

Begin by bringing to the altar a small bowl of water or a small bottle of oil. Light a candle with the intention of honoring the energy centers, or chakras, that contribute to your spiritual, mental, emotional, and physical well-being.

With one of your fingertips, place a drop of water or oil on each of your chakras in the following order, acknowledging the gift each brings. You'll begin with the top of your head and end with the bottoms of your feet in order to accentuate the experience of grounding your whole being into your physical body and daily life.

Top of head	-	spirituality
Forehead	-	intuition/intelligence
Throat	-	inner & outer voice/creativity
Heart	-	seat of compassion and love
Solar Plexus	-	feelings
Sacral	-	sexuality/generativity
Base of Spine	-	life energy
Palms of Hands	-	healing
Bottoms of Feet	-	grounding on the earth

May

MINDFULNESS

MINDFULNESS

May 1 – 8

I notice what I do with my body, I observe what I think with my mind, I experience the feelings that move through me. Mindfulness invites me to be aware of every action and experience at every moment.

෴෴

MINDFULNESS

May 9 – 16

To be mindful is to know that my hand touches water when I wash dishes, that my feet touch the ground when I walk, that my words reach across to touch someone when I speak.

๛ൠൟ

May 17 – 23

When I notice how I am and what I'm doing
in the present moment, choice becomes my
constant companion.

ଚୋଷ

MINDFULNESS

May 24 – 31

To live mindfully is to be fully alive and awake to the present moment. Once awakened to mindfulness, I recognize that the quality of each moment lived is created by *my* responses.

৪০ৰেপ

Ritual: *mindfulness*

Begin this ritual as you approach the altar. Become aware of the choice to go to the altar, of the movement of your body as you approach. Notice the sensations of sitting down and settling in. Then, look at the altar and all of its contents. Know that you are looking, notice what you see.

As you light a candle, pay attention to the experience of taking the match out of its container, striking it, and touching the flame to the wick of the candle. Blow out the match with awareness that you are blowing out a match.

Next, say aloud: *"Today I choose to be as mindful as possible, to remember who I am, where I am, and what I am doing."* Take a few moments to reflect on the power of choice.

Close the ritual by blowing out the candle, knowing that you are blowing out a candle.

June

GRATITUDE & GENEROSITY

GRATITUDE & GENEROSITY

June 1 - 7

In giving, I also receive; in receiving, I also give. The practice of gratitude and generosity challenges me both to give *and* receive without manipulation or expectation - rather, to do so freely, with an open heart.

‿❦◡

June 8 – 15

In choosing to engage the active expression of gratitude and the practice of generosity, I also engage a dynamic flow of universal energy. The more I experience the joy of giving and receiving, the more I experience outer manifestations of health, vitality, and material abundance.

୨୦୧୪

GRATITUDE & GENEROSITY

June 16 – 22

Gratitude and generosity represent, as well, a lens through which I view the world. Gratitude allows me to recognize the many gifts I have in my life, from the smallest conveniences to the most dramatic abundance. Generosity invites me to discover that there is always something more to share - that even my smile is a gift I can offer freely.

GRATITUDE & GENEROSITY

June 23 – 30

When I express gratitude and generosity actively in my life, I learn that the more gratitude I experience, the more blessings I notice - and, the more generosity I express, the more my heart is opened by my connection to others and to my world.

❧❧❧

Ritual: Gratitude & Generosity

Begin by thoughtfully choosing a vase to put near your altar. Bring a bouquet of flowers - as many or as few as you wish. Allow each flower to represent an area of gratitude in your life. As you place a flower in the vase, say aloud: *"This flower represents my gratitude for. . ."* Then go on to the next flow and the next thing for which you are grateful and repeat the above statement.

Once you have placed all the flowers in the vase, to close the ritual take a few minutes to acknowledge the bounty of life, as you also acknowldege the contribution of the flowers to your experience.

Then, later, when you feel moved to do so, give one or more of the flowers to someone else as an affirmation of your commitment to express generosity as an active part of your life.

July

Oneness

ONENESS

July 1 – 8

Oneness encompasses my whole being. I remind myself that I am part of the earth and the cosmos, that my body is made of the same elements. I acknowledge that I am part of a natural ecology, as well as a dynamic collective consciousness.

෯ඏ

ONENESS

July 9 – 16

In the awareness of collective consciousness, I am part of everything and everything is part of me. I recognize that in a world of oneness I am never alone . . . I know that I constantly contribute to and draw from this oneness and interconnection.

୫୦୯୦

ONENESS

July 17 – 23

In a context of oneness, if someone in the world suffers as part of collective consciousness, I suffer too. If someone is liberated, so am I. The tears of the person I never met are my own and so is the laughter.

ಕಾ ಡಿ

ONENESS

July 24 – 31

In a world of oneness my every word, thought, and action make a difference. I can honor the inherent relationship I have with all other life by being aware of the choices I make. My presence matters.

Ritual: Oneness

Begin by gathering together a small bowl of water, a small potted plant, something from the animal kingdom [a piece of leather, a feather, etc.], and something from the mineral kingdom [a rock, a crystal, a jewel]. Your presence at the altar represents humanity.

Next, light a candle with the intention to affirm your willingness to acknowledge the oneness that underlies each individual expression of life. Then, say the following affirmations as you place each object on the altar:

The bowl of water	-	*"I am one with the water. It is part of me, I am part of it."*
The potted plant	-	*"I am one with the plant. It is part of me, I am part of it."*
The animal object	-	*"I am one with animals. They are part of me and I am part of them."*
The mineral	-	*"I am one with minerals."*
Yourself	-	*"I find my place in the oneness of life and honor all lifeforms as my kin."*

Close the ritual by blowing out the candle and choosing to bring your awareness of oneness and kinship into your daily activities.

August

INTENTION

INTENTION

August 1 – 8

To live with intention means to make moment-to-moment, conscious choices about how I live in the world. Living with intention allows me to discover my power to play an *active* role in co-creating the life I live.

INTENTION

August 9 – 16

When I live with intention, I connect myself to the mystery of how my unspoken choices manifest in the world. I recognize that my thoughts and words, in themselves, are acts of creation. The more I am able to focus my thoughts, the more I empower the energy that moves my intentions into manifestation.

୫୦୧୪

INTENTION

August 17 – 23

Intention allows me to participate in generating the states of being, conditions, and events that enhance my life. When I live with intention, I acknowledge that my choices influence how I move through and experience my world.

☜☞

INTENTION

August 24 – 31

Knowing the power of intention, I recognize that each day offers a new opportunity to co-create my life. I choose my responses to circumstances and events, and embrace both the responsibility and the magic involved in actively manifesting my intentions.

Ritual: Intention

For this ritual, choose a special candle that will be used each day until it is completely burned, to empower an intention that you wish to create. Select a special piece of paper or a card on which you will write an outcome you want to manifest in yourself or the world.

Begin by sitting in front of the altar and mindfully write your intention on the piece of paper. As you write, open your heart as fully as possible to the choice your are making and allow yourself to be deeply aware of the power of such choice. Once you have finished writing your intention, light the special candle and read the intention out loud. Take a few moments to watch the candle flame as you reflect on your intention.

To conclude the ritual, place the written intention on your altar and blow out the candle. Each evening, light the candle again for a few minutes and read your intention aloud. Do this each evening until the candle is burned completely.

September

CREATING POSSIBILITY
WITH SYNCHRONICITY

September 1 - 7

My intentions automatically engage the realm of all possibility. Synchronicity - meaningful coincidence - brings my intentions together with that which gives them form in the world. Seemingly separate events come together actively to support and manifest my desires.

September 8 – 15

Synchronicity is the unseen force - unantici-
pated and yet timely - that brings elements
together in the dance of co-creation. As possibilities move from intention to form, synchronicity fills in the blanks, creates connec-
tions, and supports manifesting desired outcomes.

ಅಃಆ

September 16 – 22

I discover that my willingness to notice and acknowledge the meaningful coincidences in my life engages the support of synchronicity even more actively.

૪**)(**૭

September 23 – 30

Recognizing the interplay of synchronicity and the realm of all possibility, I now have a reliable means of empowering my choices and manifesting my heart's desire.

୬୬ଔଔ

Ritual: Creating Possibility with Synchronicity

Bring to the altar an object that represents an experience of synchronicity in which something happened that was unexpected and meaningful to you. An example is when you are thinking of taking a course and the mail arrives with an unsolicited brochure for just the kind of course that appeals to you.

Begin by lighting a candle and reflecting on how many synchronistic moments emerge to support you and your desired outcomes everyday. Then, say aloud the following affirmation: *"I acknowledge, empower, and welcome the activity of synchronicity in my life. I remember to be grateful for each and every time synchronicity serves me."*

Close the ritual by blowing out the candle and holding the intention to notice synchronicity at work in your life today.

October

PARADOX

PARADOX

October 1 – 8

When I stand in the presence of paradox, I recognize that there is no one truth. I discover that life is like a prism, with many truths emerging from a unified ground of being.

౮౮౬౩

PARADOX

October 9 – 16

I discover in the presence of paradox, that the more certain I am of uncertainty, the more comfortable my life becomes. As I move beyond my fixed beliefs and preconceptions, I enter a realm of dichotomies and seeming contradictions.

PARADOX

October 17 – 23

Exploring paradox more deeply invites me to
enter a dimension of experience where seemingly bad experiences may become the most
powerful openings to gifts I never knew how
to imagine.

೩೦೮೩

PARADOX

October 24 – 31

As I become more comfortable with paradox, I develop a greater understanding and compassion for a variety of perspectives. I experience an increased willingness to see the possibilities inherent in a world view that embraces "both/and" rather than "either/or."

෴ꕤ

Ritual: Paradox

This ritual invites you to affirm a paradox where life and death mutually support a special moment. To begin, bring your favorite candle to the altar, if it isn't already there. Light it and spend a few moments enjoying the play of light as it flickers from the candle's flame. Notice the color and shape of the candle itself. Take in the pleasure you experience whenever you gaze at the candle and its flame.

Next, notice how the flame feeds on the very substance of the candle to give it light. As the candle is consumed, the flame thrives. Moments of beauty often emerge from paradoxes such as these.

To close the ritual, blow out the candle with full awareness of the interplay between the life of the flame and the death of the candle. Each needs the other to fulfill its purpose.

November

ACTIVE SURRENDER

ACTIVE SURRENDER

November 1 - 7

One of the major paradoxes of living a conscious life is active surrender - which in itself requires intentional letting go. The distinction between active surrender and giving up is the difference between co-creation and a life of passive resignation.

ಉ ಖ

ACTIVE SURRENDER

November 8 – 15

The art of active surrender is itself a spiritual practice. It defies logical thinking and confronts me with the contradiction that in letting go to my deepest intention or calling, I set linear thinking aside and make room for a larger reality to support me.

ℰℴℭℬ

ACTIVE SURRENDER

November 16 – 22

By not trying to *make* things happen, and instead trusting in the workings of a larger reality, I learn that actively surrendering the need to control connects me to a source that transcends my personal understanding and grasp.

☯☮

November 23 – 30

When I learn to actively surrender on a moment-to-moment basis, I move from doing to *being*. I recognize that there is creative power in constantly aligning myself with the mystery and the wisdom of a larger, universal source.

∞ ∞

Ritual: Active Surrender

Bring a ceremonial bowl of water to the altar. To begin, light a candle and take a few moments to look at the water in the bowl. Water is a master of active surrender. Close your eyes and imagine a stream flowing by. Notice how the water in the stream flows over, around, or under any obstacle that may block its way forward. Water unerringly finds its way to its destination by actively surrendering to the contours of the landscape and flowing with the openings that naturally emerge along the way. Spend a few minutes reflecting on how water flows.

Next, say the following words aloud: *"I learn from water how to actively flow with life's challenges and opportunities."*

End by blowing out the candle and mindfully emptying the bowl of water down the sink. Observe how the water flows and finds its way to the drain. Continue to learn from the way water flows.

December

LIVING CONSCIOUSLY

LIVING CONSCIOUSLY

Decewber 1 - 8

Living consciously allows me to recall that my life is an ongoing act of creation. Within a context of *being* rather than doing, I am aware of the quality of the thoughts, words, feelings and actions I bring to myself and my world.

൭൫

December 9 – 16

When I live consciously, I expand my experience of myself and my world into realms that are both seen and unseen. I invite myself to access intuitive knowledge, and the subtle and sometimes profound realizations that arise from my deeper wisdom and from the collective consciousness in which I, and everyone else, exist.

∞

LIVING CONSCIOUSLY

December 17 – 23

Living consciously, I discover a deeper experience of *inhabiting* myself. I remember that I am both an individual and part of a larger ground of being. From this ongoing recollection I tap into a sense of presence, empowerment, and compassion that I carry with me into every moment.

೮ಆ

LIVING CONSCIOUSLY

December 24 – 31

I am aware that living consciously is, in itself,
a service both to me and to my world. Knowing I am responsible for who and what I am, I
offer my whole self to this practice.

∽◯◌

Ritual: Living Consciously

As your closing ritual for the year, this experience will be different from the others, as it takes about a half-hour and involves a ritual bath. To prepare, find three or more flowers that represent what spirituality means to you. Mindfully cut the blossoms from the stems and place them in a ceremonial bowl of water.

Next, run a bath and add aromatic bubbles or oil. Light a ceremonial candle and set it on a secure surface near your bath. Then, float the flowers on the surface of the water and get into the bath. As you settle, hold the intention that the flower blossoms will absorb any blocks you may have to living consciously and that your time in the water draws these blocks from you and transfers them to the blossoms. As the process unfolds, affirm that you willingly release any blocks and open yourself even more fully to a life lived consciously.

When you finish the bath, gather the blossoms in the bowl. Dry off and dress in a garment that is sacred. Then, with care, bring the bowl of flowers and the lit candle to your altar. Sit down and take a few moments to reflect on your experience in the bath. Say aloud, *"I affirm that I bring my whole self to the practice of living consciously next year."*

Close the ritual by blowing out the candle and committing yourself to taking the blossoms back to nature when it feels right to do so.

When it feels right, return the blossoms to nature, reaffirming your commitment to bring your whole self to the practice of living consciously.

APPENDIX

More About Rituals

The most important element in creating rituals and ceremonies is the intention to do so. Holding an intention sets a mood that you are about to participate in something that is outside the everyday - an experience that marks an occasion, place, or person as something special.

Basic to most of the rituals we have experienced is the presence of candles, sage or other incense. We usually begin by purifying the people and place where a ritual will unfold. Using the sage in this way signals that we are calling sacred space forward into our immediate awareness. Then, lighting a candle with intention - and speaking the intention aloud - energizes and enlivens the process of experiencing sacred space.

Some examples of statements that may accompany lighting or passing a lit candle from person to person include:

> *"I bring myself to this gathering and. . ."*
>
> *"I share my light with others, and I offer. . ."*
>
> *"The light from this candle represents the light of wisdom - and we call this wisdom into our gathering. . ."*

In rituals and ceremonies, candles may also be used in the same way as a speaking stick: the person holding the candle is the one who shares. At a birthday party, for example, the person who holds the ceremonial candle shares something about the person being celebrated. Similarly, at a meditation gathering, or any kind of group process, the person holding the candle shares what the experience of the gathering means to him or her.

Blowing out a candle has equal impact on a ritual, as doing so often signifies the end of the ritual, or a way of sending an intention into the world on the smoke from the candle's wick. Whenever you blow out a candle, do so mindfully.

Blessing and anointing yourself and others are powerful elements in many rituals. Blessings may be created spontaneously, taken from books, passed along from one generation to the next. Oil, water, or some other sacred liquid may be used during a blessing to anoint yourself or another. Anointing deepens the blessing, grounding it in the physical world. Looking into the eyes of someone you are anointing and blessing is a powerful experience - a deeply intimate sharing - and can bring a ritual alive.

Following are some examples of generic blessings. Obviously, you'll want to create new ones that convey the spirit and intention of the particular ritual or ceremony you are putting together:

> *"May your heart be filled with gratitude as you receive the blessings of this day, and may your spirit be nourished by all that this awareness brings."*

> *"My heart to your heart, my soul to your soul. May we know the oneness that unites us."*

Often, we anoint one another by putting oil or water on the forehead with a fingertip as we say the blessing. At other times, we may touch the heartspace of the person receiving the blessing. The important thing is that the touch be sacred and the person receiving it be comfortable.

When preparing for a ritual, you can be as creative as you want in setting the space. For example, as elements in a ceremony you may choose a special cloth to cover a table, meaningful objects to place ceremoniously on surfaces that call to you, such as candles, chimes, music, inspirational pictures and readings. You may also choose to wear clothing that symbolizes that you are entering a sacred experience. For example, you might have a particular shirt or garment that you wear especially for this kind of occasion.

What follows are some general categories of ritual and ceremony, and a few examples of each. We offer these examples in the hope that they will spark your own creativity and intuition in bringing ritual and ceremony more actively and richly into your daily life:

Honoring Physical Space

This kind of ritual can be used to bless a new house, apartment, office, or other space, or to say good-bye to a space you are leaving.

Light a candle and, in a fireproof container, light some sage. Turn to the four corners of the room while honoring the four directions, as well as what is above and what is below. Different traditions have different meanings for each direction. For example, in some traditions, when you turn to the north, you honor the elements of earth and the quality of wisdom. Next, turn to the south and honor water and trust. Then, turning east you honor air and the quality of illumination, while turning west honors fire and introspection. (In another tradition, north is the earth, south is fire, east is air, and west is water.) Then, take a moment to acknowledge what is above and what is below. If you choose to honor the directions in this way, assign whatever elements and meanings related to each direction that make the most sense in your worldview.

Welcome, or say good-bye, to the spirit of the room and request that the space be blessed with love and light. Each person present can hold the candle while speaking their blessings or gratitude to the space. For example, in a building that had been used for classes and workshops, a group of people could come together to release the space for new activities. Each person could take the ceremonial candle in turn and talk about their experiences in the space over the years, thanking it, and then releasing it to new activities.

To close the ritual, a chime or bell may be rung while everyone present affirms in their minds and hearts the manifestation of the ceremonial intention.

Family Ritual

As an ongoing ritual for the family, or for a holiday, celebration, or special family event, choose a vase and place it in a location of honor. Fill it with water and have each member of the family bring a flower to add to the vase. Each flower symbolizes that person's contribution to the life of the family, or to the intention of the family celebration. Over time, as flowers die, members of the family remove them and add new ones, understanding that each new flower symbolizes the ongoing vitality and renewal of the family's life.

If the flowers are bought in a store, choose them individually with an awareness of the role they will play in honoring the family or particular occasion. If you pick them from a field or garden, choose them for the qualities and acknowledge their contribution in serving the family in this sacred way. As you discard the flowers, when possible, put them on or bury them in the earth so that they continue their contribution by nourishing other plant life as they decay.

Rights of Passage

Rituals that honor rites of passage may be used to acknowledge any kind of life transition, achievement, or other important experience that marks a person's, or group's, journey from where they were to a new way of being or new life condition.

Ritual to Honor Death

In this ritual, find a container that can hold a small candle that can be replaced from time to time. Lighting the candle honors the spark of light, the spirit of the person who has died. As you light the candle, say something that acknowledges the person's presence in the world, that they had an impact and will be remembered. Take a few moments to recall the person's face, voice, or other characteristics that come to mind. When you do this, you honor the person's importance in your life.

When you blow out the candle, offer a prayer for the person in whatever way makes sense to you. You can send them love, wishes for a good afterlife journey, or any other blessing or wish you want to convey. Extinguishing the candle acknowledges that life ends for us all, as it has for this person.

When the candle burns down, replace it and continue the ritual for as many months or years as you want. Each time you replace the candle, you affirm that the deceased person has become an ancestor whose life experience, wisdom, and presence in the world has prepared the way for, and supported, all who follow.

Ritual to Honor an Elder

This ritual may be used to honor and celebrate a person who, by virtue of age and experience, is an elder. When setting the time and place for the ceremony, request in advance that each person bring a small container of water from their community. The water may be taken from the ocean, a lake or stream, a fountain or other source. Also, invite all participants to prepare a brief blessing or statement about how the elder's wisdom and life experience have been meaningful in the person's life.

Before beginning the ceremony, have a large bowl in which you will put the water each participant brings. When all are gathered, have the elder sit in a place of honor within the circle of those present. Have one of the members of the circle come forward and remove socks or shoes the elder may be wearing. Then, have each person pour their water into the bowl and place the bowl by the feet of the elder. Invite someone to wash and dry the elder's feet with this sacred water and pieces of cloth chosen especially for the ceremony. Next, go around the circle and have each person speak their blessing.

To close the ritual, and if it is convenient, return the water to the earth, or to a body of water of some kind. If not, dispose of it in whatever way honors the role it has played in the ritual. Finally, have each person approach the elder individually, looking into the eyes of the elder and bowing to the wisdom and life experience the elder has attained.

Honoring the Transition into Adulthood

FOR GIRLS

To prepare this ritual, women who are close to a girl who is either 13 years old, or who has begun to menstruate, gather the following materials: A pouch to be worn around the girl's neck that contains sacred objects, totems that each woman will give the girl during the ritual. These objects will be chosen by each woman specifically to represent the transition from girlhood to now living as a woman. Ahead of time, have each woman think about what wishes and blessings she will want to share with the girl at the end of the ceremony. Ask the girl to think ahead of time about an affirmation of commitment she will speak that conveys her own wishes and values about taking her place as a woman in her community. Also, have a candle for each woman and a special candle of honor for the girl.

Gather together in a circle, giving the girl a place of honor. Each woman lights a candle, one at a time, with the intention that in doing so, she brings her presence and her woman's wisdom to the circle and the ceremony. Give the special candle to the girl and, as she lights it, she holds the intention that she is present to receive the woman's wisdom from her elders.

Next, whoever has made or brought the pouch places it in front of the girl, on a table or on the floor. Then, one at a time, each woman shows the girl the object she has brought, places her gift in the pouch, and tells the girl why it was chosen especially for her transition into womanhood. Then, when all the objects have been put in the pouch, one of the women puts it around the girl's neck. It symbolizes the gifts of woman's wisdom that she now carries with her always.

The girl speaks her affirmation of commitment to the women present. Each woman now speaks in turn, sharing her wishes and blessings for the girl. When all have spoken, the girl is welcomed into the circle of women.

For Boys

This ritual is for boys who are 13, or in some other way are identified as making their transition into manhood. The older men each bring a small object that is a totem representing the qualities of manhood, to go into the waist pouch that will be given to the boy. Each man also brings a blessing and whatever male wisdom he wants to share with the boy. Ahead of time, the men think about what blessings they want to convey to the boy at the end of the ritual, and the boy creates a statement of manhood, his commitment about how he wants to be, and the values he wants to hold and express.

This ritual also includes a drum and one ceremonial candle. To begin, the men gather in a circle with the boy in the center, with his waist pouch already on. The eldest man in the group lights the candle and places it at the boy's feet. Each man then hands his object to the boy, as he shares with it represents. Then, the boy places the object into the waist pouch.

One by one, each man drums, as he shares with the boy his blessings and words of wisdom to support his journey through manhood. Finally, the drum is handed to the boy who taps it as he walks around the inside of the circle, making eye contact with each man as he passes by. In this way, he ritually receives his blessings, accepts his role as a man in his family and community, and claims his participation in male wisdom. He puts the drum in the center of the circle, and takes his place in the outer circle with the other men. The eldest man then concludes the ceremony by blowing out the candle.

Continuing the Journey. . .

It has been our privilege to share this reflective meditation process with you. We hope it has nourished, inspired, and supported your spiritual journey throughout this year.

We invite you to revisit these themes often, perhaps by going through the process again in the coming year. It has been our experience that reconnecting with these themes brings them increasingly more alive. When we recall these spiritual concepts and our reflections about them, they become tangible and available states of mind and ways of being.

May your experience as an irreplaceable part of a dynamic universe increase in powerful and satisfying ways, wherever your journey may lead.

About the Authors

NANCY J. NAPIER, L.M.F.T., is a psychotherapist and hypnotherapist in private practice in New York City. Her other books include *Sacred Practices for Conscious Living*, *Getting Through the Day*, and *Recreating Your Self*. Nancy has an extensive background in spirituality, meditation practices, and applying spiritual principles to everyday life, which she brings to her work with individuals and couples. In her work as a trauma specialist, Nancy draws on Somatic Experiencing, EMDR, Thought Field Therapy, and other resource-based approaches. She offers workshops for professionals and the public on subjects including the transpersonal dimensions of therapy, healing from abuse, being fully in the present moment with what is as it is, living with intention, accessing future possibilities, and enhancing mindful living.

CAROLYN M. TRICOMI, Ph.D., is a Professor of Counseling at John Jay College of Criminal Justice, the City University of New York. She is a senior trainer for the College, leading Human Dignity seminars for police both nationally and internationally, with a focus in Eastern Europe, Southeast Asia, and Southern Africa. Carolyn has an extensive background in spirituality and transpersonal approaches to psychotherapy which she brings to her work with individuals and couples in private practice. Her experience bringing spiritual principles into everyday life is reflected in her work with addictions and abuse. She facilitates workshops on meditation and Breathwork, as well as leading women's circles that focus on ritual, self-healing, and living in the present moment.

For information about books, workshops, and audio tapes, contact **Lotus Blossom Press, P.O. Box 153, New York, New York 10024.**